WHAT ABOUT
THE CHURCH?

Other booklets from *Questions of Life* include:

Other booklets from *Searching Issues* include:

What About the Church?

NICKY GUMBEL

Alpha

Text cartoons by Charlie Mackesy
Cover artwork by Glenn Andrews

ISBN 1 84291 204 6

Published by
KINGSWAY COMMUNICATIONS LTD
Lottbridge Drove, Eastbourne BN23 6NT, England.
Email: books@kingsway.co.uk
Printed in Canada

Contents

What about the Church?

Abraham Lincoln once said, 'If all the people who fell asleep in church on Sunday morning were laid out end to end ... they would be a great deal more comfortable.' Hard pews, unsingable tunes, enforced silence and excruciating boredom are just a few ingredients that make up the common image of church on Sunday. It is seen as an experience through which to grit one's teeth stoically until the aroma of gravy brightens up the prospects of the day. A vicar was taking a small boy around his church and showing him the memorials. 'These are the names of those who died in the Services.' The boy asked, 'Did they die at the morning service or at the evening service?'

Some associate the word 'church' with the clergy. Somebody who is entering the ordained ministry is said to be 'going into the church'. Those embarking on such a career are often viewed with suspicion, and the assumption is made that they are absolutely incapable of doing anything else. Hence a recent advert in the church press: 'Are you forty-five and getting nowhere? Why not consider the Christian ministry?' Clergy are sometimes perceived as: 'Six days invisible, one day incomprehensible!'

Others associate the word 'church' with a particular denomination. For example, Baptists or Methodists. Still others associate the word 'church' with church buildings. They assume that to be a minister you must be interested in church architecture, and when they go on holiday they send their vicar a picture of the local church building. I heard one clergyman imploring his congregation not to send him postcards of churches, telling them he had very little interest in church architecture!

Some tick off 'church' on their list of yearly duties, somewhere between visiting Great Aunt Edna in Hove and making a cake for the village fete. The attitude of others is summed up in a ditty:

So when I've nothing else to do,
I think I'll pay a visit,
So when at last I'm carried in,
The Lord won't say, 'Who is it?'

There may be an element of truth in some of these views. However, many Christians are seeking to bury this image of the church as it is wholly inadequate when compared to the picture of the church in the New Testament. Many churches are now creating a wonderfully warm and outward-going Christian family which is much closer to the biblical picture. In the New Testament there are over 100 images or analogies of the church, and in this booklet I want to look at five which are central to the understanding of the church.

THE PEOPLE OF GOD

The church is made up of people. The Greek word for church, *ekklesia*, means 'an assembly' or 'gathering of people'. Sometimes the New Testament refers to the universal church (eg, Ephesians 3:10, 21; 5:23, 25, 27, 29, 32). The universal church consists of all those worldwide and down the ages who profess or have professed the name of Christ.

Baptism is a visible mark of being a member of the church. It is also a visible sign of what it means to be a Christian. It signifies cleansing from sin (1 Corinthians 6:11), dying and rising with Christ to a new life (Romans 6:3–5; Colossians 2:12) and the living water which the Holy Spirit brings to our lives (1 Corinthians 12:13). Jesus himself commanded his followers to go and make disciples and to baptise them (Matthew 28:19).

The universal Christian church is vast. According to the *Encyclopaedia Britannica*, it has nearly 1,900,000,000 adherents in 270 countries, consisting of 34 per cent of the world population. In many parts of the world, where there are extreme and oppressive regimes, the church is persecuted. In these parts it is mainly underground but, by all accounts, very strong. In the

Third World it is growing rapidly. In some countries, such as Kenya, it is estimated that 80 per cent of the population are now professed Christians. On the other hand, in the free world the church has largely been in decline. According to a survey carried out by *Christian Research*, in the course of the 1990s a million people stopped going to church on an average Sunday in Britain. At one time the West was sending missionaries to the Third World. However, I remember that when I was in Cambridge, three Ugandan missionaries came there to preach the gospel. It struck me then how much the world had changed in the last 150 years and that England needed missionaries as much as anywhere else.

In the New Testament, Paul speaks of local churches, for example the 'Galatian churches' (1 Corinthians 16:1), 'the churches in the province of Asia' (1 Corinthians 16:19) and 'all the churches of Christ' (Romans 16:16). Even those local churches seem at times to have broken down into smaller gatherings which met in homes (Romans 16:5; 1 Corinthians 16:19).

In effect, there seems to have been three types of gathering in the Bible: the large, the medium-sized and the small. These are practical levels at which we experience what the church is: the celebration, congregation and cell. All three are important and complement each other.

The celebration is a large gathering of Christians. This may take place every Sunday in big churches, or when a number of small churches come together for worship. In the Old Testament, the people of God came together for special celebrations with a festive atmosphere at Passover, Pentecost or at the New Year. Today, large gatherings of Christians provide inspiration. Through them many can recapture a vision of the greatness of

God and a profound sense of worship. These gatherings of hundreds of Christians together can restore confidence to those who have felt isolated and provide a visible presence of the church in the community. However, on their own such gatherings are not enough. They are not places where Christian friendships can easily develop.

The congregation, in this sense, is a medium-sized gathering. The size makes it possible to know most people and be known by most. It is a place where lasting Christian friendships can be made. It is also a place where the gifts and ministries of the Spirit can be exercised in an atmosphere of love and acceptance, where people are free to risk making mistakes. It is a place where individuals can learn, for example, to give talks, lead worship, pray for the sick, develop the gift of prophecy and learn to pray out loud.

The third level of meeting is the 'cell', which we call the 'small group'. These groups consist of two to twelve people who gather to study the Bible and pray together. It is in these groups that the closest friendships in the church are made. They are characterised by confidentiality (that we can speak openly without fear of gossip), intimacy (that it is a group where we can speak about what really matters in our lives) and account-ability (that we are willing to listen to and learn from one another).

THE FAMILY OF GOD

When we receive Jesus Christ into our lives, we become children of God (John 1:12). This is what gives the church its unity. We have God as our Father, Jesus Christ as our Saviour and the Holy Spirit as our indweller. We all belong to one family. Although brothers and sisters may squabble and fall out or not see each other for long periods of time, they still remain brothers and sisters. Nothing can end that relationship. So the church is one, even though it often appears to be divided.

This does not mean that we settle for disunity. Jesus prayed for his followers 'that they may be one' (John 17:11). Paul says, 'Make every effort to keep the unity of the Spirit' (Ephesians 4:3). Like a divided family we should always strive for reconciliation. The incarnation demands a visible expression of our invisible unity. Of course, this unity should not be achieved at the expense of truth but, as the Medieval writer Rupertus Meldenius put it, 'On the necessary points, unity; on the questionable points, liberty; in everything, love.'

At every level we should seek unity – in the small group, congregation and celebration; within our denomination and between denominations. This unity is brought about as theologians and church leaders get together to debate and work through theological differences. But it is also achieved, often more effectively, by ordinary Christians getting together to worship and work together. The nearer we come to Christ, the nearer we come together. David Watson used a striking illustration. He said:

> When you travel by air and the plane lifts off the ground, the walls and hedges which may seem large and impressive at ground level, at once lose their significance. In the same way, when the power of the Holy Spirit lifts us up together into the conscious realisation of the presence of Jesus, the barriers between us become unimportant. Seated with Christ in the heavenly places, the differences between Christians can often seem petty and marginal.[1]

Since we have the same Father, we are brothers and sisters and are all called to love one another. John puts it very clearly:

If we say we love God yet hate a brother or sister, we are liars. For any of us who do not love a brother or sister, whom we have seen, cannot love God, whom we have not seen. And he has given us this command: Those who love God must also love one another. Everyone who believes that Jesus is the Christ is born of God, and everyone who loves the father loves his child as well (1 John 4:20 – 5:1).

The Pope's personal preacher, Father Raniero Cantalamessa, addressing a gathering of thousands from many different denominations said, 'When Christians quarrel we say to God: "Choose between us and them." But the Father loves *all* his children. We should say, "We accept as our brothers all those whom you receive as your children." '

We are called to fellowship with one another. The Greek word *koinonia* means 'having in common' or 'sharing'. It is the word used for the marital relationship, the most intimate between human beings. Our fellowship is with God (Father, Son and Holy Spirit – 1 John 1:3; 2 Corinthians 13:14) and with one another (1 John 1:7). Christian fellowship cuts across race, colour, education, background and every other cultural barrier. There is a level of friendship in the church which I have certainly never experienced outside the church.

John Wesley said, 'The New Testament knows nothing of solitary religion.' We are called to fellowship with one another. It is not an optional extra. There are two things we simply cannot do alone. We cannot marry alone and we cannot be a Christian alone. Professor C.E.B. Cranfield put it like this: 'The freelance Christian, who would be a Christian but is too superior to belong to the visible Church upon earth in one of its forms, is simply a contradiction in terms.'

The writer of Hebrews urges his readers, 'Let us consider how we may spur one another on towards love and good deeds. Let us not give up meeting together, as some are in the habit of doing, but let us encourage one another – and all the more as you see the Day approaching' (Hebrews 10:24–25). Often Christians lose their love for the Lord and their enthusiasm for their faith because they neglect fellowship.

One man who found himself in this position was visited by a wise old Christian. They sat in front of the coal fire in the sitting room. The old man never spoke, but went to the coal fire and picked out a red-hot coal with some tongs and put it on the hearth. He still said nothing. In a few minutes the coal had lost its glow. Then he picked it up and put it back in the fire. After a short time it began to glow again. The old man still said nothing at all but, as he got up to leave, the other man knew exactly why he had lost his fervour – a Christian out of fellowship is like a coal out of the fire. Martin Luther wrote in his diary, 'At home in my house there is no warmth or vigour in me, but in the church when the multitude is gathered together, a fire is kindled in my heart and it breaks its way through.'

THE BODY OF CHRIST

Paul had been persecuting the Christian church when he encountered Jesus Christ on the road to Damascus. Jesus said to him, 'Saul, Saul, why do you persecute *me*?' (Acts 9:4, italics mine). Paul had never met Jesus before so he must have realised that Jesus was saying that, in persecuting Christians, he was persecuting Jesus himself. It may well be that from his encounter Paul realised that the church was, in effect, the body of

Christ. 'He calls the church Christ,' wrote the sixteenth-century reformer, Calvin. We Christians are Christ to the world. As the old hymn says:

> He has no hands but our hands
> To do His work today;
> He has no feet but our feet
> To lead men in His way;
> He has no voice but our voice
> To tell men how He died;
> He has no help but our help
> To lead them to His side.

Paul develops this analogy in 1 Corinthians 12. The body is a unit (v. 12), yet this unity does not mean uniformity. 'Those who are members of one another become as diverse as the hand and the ear. That is why the worldlings are so monotonously alike compared with the almost fantastic variety of the saints. Obedience is the road to freedom, humility the road to pleasure, unity the road to personality.'[2] There are 'many parts' and they are all different with 'different kinds of gifts' and 'different kinds of working' (vv. 4–6).

What then should our attitude be to other parts of the body of Christ?

Paul deals with two wrong attitudes. First, he speaks to those who feel inferior and who feel that they have nothing to offer. For example, Paul says the foot may feel inferior to the hand or the ear inferior to the eye (vv. 14–19). It is a human tendency to feel envious of others.

It is easy to look round the church and feel inferior and therefore not needed. As a result we do nothing. In fact we are all needed. God has given gifts 'to each one' (v. 7). The term 'to each one' runs through 1 Corinthians 12 as a common thread.

Each person has at least one gift which is absolutely necessary for the proper functioning of the body. Unless each of us plays the part God has designed for us, the church will not be able to function as it should. In the following verses, Paul turns to those who feel superior (vv. 21–25) and are saying to others, 'I don't need you.' Again, Paul points out the folly of this position. A body without a foot is not as effective as it might be (see v. 21). Often the parts which are unseen are even more important than those with a higher profile.

The right attitude is one which recognises that we are all in it together. We are all part of a team – each part affects the whole. From Plato onwards, the 'I' has been the personality that gives unity to the body. We do not say, 'My head has an ache.' We say, 'I have a headache.' So it is with the body of Christ. 'If one part suffers, every part suffers with it; if one part is honoured, every part rejoices with it' (v. 26).

Every Christian is a part of the church. John Wimber was once approached by a member of his congregation who had met somebody in great need. After the Sunday service this man told John Wimber of his frustration in trying to get help. 'This man needed a place to stay, food and support while he gets on his feet and looks for a job,' he said. 'I am really frustrated. I tried telephoning the church office, but no one could see me and they couldn't help me. I finally ended up having to let him stay with me for the week! Don't you think the church should take care of people like this?' John Wimber says he thought for a moment and then said, 'It looks like *the church* did.'

The problem with the church is that for years it has either been pulpit-centred or altar-centred, according to our different traditions. In both situations the dominant role has been played by the minister or the priest. As Michael Green said, commenting on the spectacular spread of the Pentecostal churches in South America, 'It is … due to many causes, but not least to the fact that it is predominantly a lay church'[3] (i.e. run by the people).

A HOLY TEMPLE

The only church building the New Testament speaks about is a building made of people. Paul says that the Christians are 'being built together to become a dwelling in which God lives by his Spirit' (Ephesians 2:22). Jesus is the chief cornerstone. He is the one who founded the church and around whom the church is built. The foundations are 'the apostles and prophets' and the result is a holy temple made of 'living stones'.

In the Old Testament the tabernacle (and later the temple) was central to Israel's worship. This was the place where people went to meet with God. At times his presence filled the temple (1 Kings 8:11) and especially the Holy of Holies. Access to his presence was strictly limited (see Hebrews 9).

Through his death on the cross for us, Jesus opened up access to the Father for all believers all the time. His presence is no longer confined to a physical temple; now he is present by his Spirit with all believers. His presence is especially sensed when Christians gather together (Matthew 18:20). His new temple is the church which is 'a dwelling in which God lives by his Spirit'.

Gordon Fee, Professor of NT at Regent's College, Canada, has written:

Presence is a delicious word – because it points to one of our truly great gifts. Nothing else can take the place of presence, not gifts, not telephone calls, not pictures, not mementos, nothing. Ask the person who has lost a lifelong mate what they miss the most; the

17

answer is invariably 'presence'. When we are ill, we don't need soothing words nearly as much as we need loved ones to be present. What makes a shared life – games, walks, concerts, outings, and a myriad of other things – so pleasurable? Presence.[4]

The presence of God was what Adam and Eve lost in the Garden of Eden. But God promised that he would restore his presence. In the Old Testament his presence came into the temple. His glory filled the temple. That is why the people of Israel longed to go there. 'How lovely is your dwelling-place, O Lord Almighty! My soul yearns, even faints, for the courts of the Lord; my heart and my flesh cry out for the living God' (Psalm 84:1). One of the reasons the exile was such a disaster is that the people of God were away from God's presence. Then God promised that one day he was going to make his presence more widely known. On the day of Pentecost when the Spirit of God was poured out, the presence of God came to live among his people.

Paul writes of individual Christians, 'Do you not know that your bodies are temples of the Holy Spirit, who is in you, whom you have received from God?' (1 Corinthians 6:19). But more often he writes that the church, the gathered community of Christians, is the temple of the Holy Spirit. That is where God lives by his Spirit.

Under the Old Covenant (before Jesus), access to the Father was through a priest (Hebrews 4:14), who made sacrifices on behalf of believers. Now Jesus, our great high priest, has made the supreme sacrifice of his own life on our behalf. Jesus 'appeared once for all at the end of the ages to do away with sin by the sacrifice of himself' (Hebrews 9:26). We do not need to make further sacrifices for our sins. Rather, we need to be constantly reminded of his sacrifice for us. At the service of

Holy Communion, sometimes called the Lord's Supper or the Eucharist, we remember his sacrifice with thanksgiving and partake of its benefits.

As we receive the bread and wine we look in four directions:

We look back with thanks
The bread and wine remind us of the broken body and shed blood of Jesus Christ on the cross. As we receive Communion we look back to the cross with thankfulness that he died for us so that our sins could be forgiven and our guilt removed (Matthew 26:26–28).

We look forward with anticipation
Jesus could have left us some other way to remember his death, but he chose to leave us a meal. A meal is often a way in which we celebrate great occasions. One day in heaven we are going to celebrate for eternity at 'the wedding supper' of Jesus Christ (Revelation 19:9). The bread and wine are a foretaste of this (Luke 22:16; 1 Corinthians 11:26).

We look around at the Christian family
Drinking from one cup and eating the one loaf symbolises our unity in Christ. 'Because there is one loaf, we, who are many, are one body, for we all partake of the one loaf' (1 Corinthians 10:17). That is why we do not receive the bread and the wine on our own. Eating and drinking together in this way should not only remind us of our unity, it should strengthen that unity as we look around at our brothers and sisters for whom Christ died.

We look up in expectation

The bread and wine represent the body and blood of Jesus. Jesus promised to be with us by his Spirit after his death, and especially wherever Christians meet together: 'Where two or three come together in my name, there am I with them' (Matthew 18:20). So as we receive Communion we look up to Jesus with expectancy. In our experience, we have found that on such occasions there are sometimes conversions, healing and powerful encounters with the presence of Christ.

THE BRIDE OF CHRIST

This is one of the most beautiful analogies of the church in the New Testament. Paul says when speaking of the husband and wife relationship: 'This is a profound mystery – but I am talking about Christ and the church' (Ephesians 5:32). As the Old Testament speaks about God being a husband to Israel (Isaiah 54:1–8), so in the New Testament Paul speaks about Christ being a husband to the church and the model of every human marriage relationship. So he tells husbands to love their wives 'just as Christ loved the church and gave himself up for her to make her holy, cleansing her by the washing with water through the word, and to present her to himself as a radiant church, without stain or wrinkle or any other blemish, but holy and blameless' (Ephesians 5:25–27).

This picture of the holy and radiant church may not accord entirely with the present condition of the church, but we get a glimpse here of what Jesus intends for his church. One day Jesus will return in glory. In the Book of Revelation, John has a vision of the church, 'the new Jerusalem, coming down out of heaven from God, prepared as a bride beautifully dressed for her husband' (Revelation 21:2). Today the church is small and weak. One day we shall see the church as Jesus intends it to be. In the meantime, we must try to bring our experiences as close as possible to the vision of the New Testament.

Our response to Christ's love for us should be one of love for him. The way we show our love for him is by living in holiness and purity – being a bride fit for him and fulfilling his purpose for us. This is his intention for us. This is how his purposes for us will be fulfilled. We are to be changed and to be made beautiful until we are fit to be his bride.

Moreover, his purpose for his church is that we 'may declare the praises of him who called you out of darkness into his wonderful light' (1 Peter 2:9). Declaring his praises involves both worship and witness. Our worship is the expression of our love and reverence for God with our whole beings – heart, mind and bodies. This is the purpose for which we were made. As the Westminster catechism puts it, 'The chief end of man is to glorify God and enjoy him for ever.'

Our witness is our response of love towards other people. He has called us to tell others the good news and draw them into his church – to declare his wonderful deeds to the people around us. In both our worship and our witness we need to find a contemporary expression for eternal truths. God does not change; neither does the gospel. We cannot change our doctrine or our message just to suit passing fashions. But the way in which we worship and the way in which we communicate the gospel must resonate with modern men and women. For many this will mean contemporary music and contemporary language.

If the church was closer to the New Testament images, church services would be far from dull and boring. Indeed, they should be very exciting and sometimes are. The church is made up of the people belonging to God, who are bound together in love as a family with Christ in their midst. They represent Christ to the world, loving their Lord as a bride loves the bridegroom, and being loved by him as a bride is loved by the bridegroom. What a place to be – it should be near heaven on earth.

A young couple who have recently come to faith in Christ wrote:

> We have been coming to church for a year now and it already feels like home. The atmosphere of love, friendship and excitement is impossible to find elsewhere. The joy of it far exceeds any evening at a pub, party or restaurant … I am shocked to say (although I continue to enjoy all three). Both of us find that Sunday's service and Wednesday's gathering are two high points of the week. At times, it feels like coming up for air, especially as by Wednesday it is easy to be drowning in the deep waters of working life! If we miss either, we feel somehow 'diluted'. Of course, we can keep talking to God together and alone, but I feel that the act of meeting together is the bellows that keep on fanning the flames of our faith.

Notes

1. David Watson, *I Believe in the Church* (Hodder & Stoughton, 1978).
2. C. S. Lewis, *Fern Seeds and Elephants* (Fontana, 1975).
3. Michael Green, *Called to Serve* (Hodder & Stoughton, 1964). With thanks to the Curtis Brown Agency.
4. Gordon Fee, *Paul, The Spirit and the People of God* (Hodder & Stoughton, 1997).

Study Guide

1. What definition would you give to the word 'church'?
2. How does the Greek word for church help to explain what it is all about (p. 9)?
3. What are the three types of Christian gathering referred to in the New Testament (p. 10)? What are the distinctive roles of each one?
4. 'The church is one, even though it often appears divided' (p. 12). What can we do about the things that divide us?
5. '… we cannot be a Christian alone' (p. 13). Do you agree? Why?
6. What exactly do you need your fellow Christians for (p. 13f.)? In what specific ways do they need you?
7. What does 'the dwelling place of God' (p. 17) actually mean in practice?
8. How can the service of Holy Communion be entered into more fully (pp. 19f.)?
9. In what ways do you think the church falls short of the pattern described in the New Testament (p. 20f.)? What might we do to change things for the better?

Alpha

This book is an Alpha resource. The Alpha course is a practical introduction to the Christian faith initiated by Holy Trinity Brompton in London, and now being run by thousands of churches throughout the UK as well as overseas.

For more information on Alpha, and details of tapes, videos and training manuals, contact the Alpha office, Holy Trinity Brompton on 0207 581 8255, (home page: http://www.alpha.org), or STL, PO Box 300, Kingstown Broadway, Carlisle, Cumbria CA3 0QS.

Alpha Hotline for telephone orders:
0845 7581 278 (all calls at local rate)

To order from overseas:
Tel +44 1228 611749
Fax +44 1228 514949

Email: alpha@stl.org

Alpha

Alpha titles available

Alpha: Questions of Life   The Alpha course in book form. In fifteen compelling chapters Nicky Gumbel points the way to an authentic Christianity which is exciting and relevant to todays world. Also available as booklets.

Searching Issues   The seven issues most often raised by participants on the Alpha course: suffering, other religions, sex before marriage, the New Age, homosexuality, science and Christianity, and the Trinity. Also available as booklets.

A Life Worth Living   What happens after Alpha? Based on the book of Philippians, this is an invaluable next step for those who have just completed the Alpha course, and for anyone eager to put their faith on a firm biblical footing.

How to Run the Alpha Course: Telling Others   The theological principles and the practical details of how courses are run. Each alternate chapter consists of a testimony of someone whose life has been changed by God through an Alpha course.

Challenging Lifestyle   Studies in the Sermon on the Mount showing how Jesus' teaching flies in the face of modern lifestyle and presents us with a radical alternative.

The Heart of Revival   Ten Bible studies based on the book of Isaiah, drawing out important truths for today by interpreting some of the teaching of the Old Testament prophet Isaiah. The book seeks to understand what revival might mean and how we can prepare to be part of it.

30 Days   Nicky Gumbel selects thirty passages from the Old and New Testament which can be read over thirty days. It is designed for those on an Alpha course and others who are interested in beginning to explore the Bible.

Why Jesus?   A booklet – given to all participants at the start of the Alpha course. 'The clearest, best illustrated and most challenging short presentation of Jesus that I know.' – Michael Green

All titles are by Nicky Gumbel, who is vicar of
Holy Trinity Brompton